AT FIRST LIGHT

40 PRAYERS AND QUOTATIONS FROM THE BAHÁ'Í WRITINGS

Dedicated to Zorion, Zavian, and Coralie.

We love you always and we hope that these quotations and prayers comfort and inspire you throughout your lives.

~Mom and Dad

Copyright © 2018 Chelsea Lee Smith. All Rights Reserved.

Front cover design by Michelle Cormack. Back cover design by Shimoné Mackie.

Photograph on back cover taken by Sara Macdonald in 2015.

Special thanks to Karyn Robarts for her contribution to recording the "At First Light" music.

No part of this book may be reproduced in any form including by any electronic or mechanical means without written consent of the author giving permission.

Description: "At First Light" is a collection of 19 quotations revealed by Bahá'u'lláh and 19 Bahá'í prayers, with an extra quotation and prayer for Ayyám-i-Há. The CD of the same name is available on cdbaby.com and features vocals, acoustic guitar and hand percussion by Soulrise Melodies - a musical duo consisting of husband and wife, Zafar and Chelsea Smith. The simple and uplifting melodies have been created especially for use during family prayers, children's classes, and devotional gatherings. The musical album and this book have been reviewed and approved by the National Spiritual Assembly of the Bahá'ís of Australia.

Free downloads are available at SoulriseMelodies.com including:

- Guitar chords
- Printable activity pages
- "Family Virtue Time" bonus track

AT FIRST LIGHT

1. Essence of cleanliness
2. Pure heart
3. Source of courage
4. Guide me
5. Observe courtesy
6. Make this youth radiant
7. He should forgive
8. I beg Thee to forgive me
9. Deal ye one with another
10. Enable me to grow
11. Generous in prosperity
12. Repair for refuge
13. Gentle winds
14. Thy name is my healing
15. Benefit mankind
16. These lovely children
17. Blissful joy
18. I have wakened
19. Kindly tongue
20. Aid Thou Thy trusted servants
21. Flame of love
22. Make Thy beauty
23. Observe My commandments
24. To be steadfast
25. Be patient
26. Say: God sufficeth
27. Reconcile their differences
28. Refresh and gladden
29. Sanctity of thy pledge
30. Assist Thy loved ones
31. Arise thou to serve
32. I have detached myself
33. Yield Him thanks
34. Voice my thanks
35. Beautify your tongues
36. I am a little child
37. Unity is firmly established
38. Unite the hearts
39. Ayyám-i-Há quotation
40. My fire and my light

These numbers correspond to the tracks on the CD.

<u>At First Light</u> was inspired by the following quotation:

"Every day at first light, ye gather the Bahá'í children together and teach them the communes and prayers. This is a most praiseworthy act, and bringeth joy to the children's hearts: that they should, at every morn, turn their faces toward the Kingdom and make mention of the Lord and praise His Name, and in the sweetest of voices, chant and recite. These children are even as young plants, and teaching them the prayers is as letting the rain pour down upon them, that they may wax tender and fresh, and the soft breezes of the love of God may blow over them, making them to tremble with joy."

'Abdu'l-Bahá, Selections from the Writings of 'Abdu'l-Bahá, p. 139

Essence of cleanliness   1

Be ye
the very essence
of cleanliness
amongst mankind.

Bahá'u'lláh, The Kitáb-i-Aqdas, p. 46

2   Pure heart

He is God!
O God, my God!
Bestow upon me a pure heart
like unto a pearl.

'Abdu'l-Bahá, Bahá'í Prayers, p. 29

Source of courage

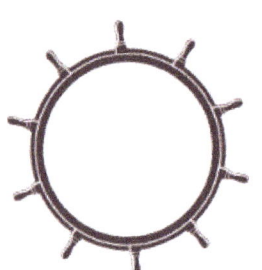

The source of courage
and power is
the promotion of the Word of God,
and steadfastness
in His love.

Bahá'u'lláh, Tablets of Bahá'u'lláh, p. 153

Guide me

O God, guide me, protect me,
make of me a shining lamp
and a brilliant star.
Thou art the Mighty and
the Powerful.

'Abdu'l-Bahá, Bahá'í Prayers, p. 36

Observe courtesy   5

...observe courtesy,
for above all else
it is the prince of virtues.

Bahá'u'lláh, Tablets of Bahá'u'lláh, p. 88

6   Make this youth radiant

O Lord! Make this youth radiant, and confer Thy bounty upon this poor creature. Bestow upon him knowledge, grant him added strength at the break of every morn and guard him within the shelter of Thy protection so that he may be freed from error, may devote himself to the service of Thy Cause, may guide the wayward, lead the hapless, free the captives and awaken the heedless, that all may be blessed with Thy remembrance and praise. Thou art the Mighty and the Powerful.

'Abdu'l-Bahá, Bahá'í Prayers, p. 36

7 He should forgive

He should forgive the sinful, and never despise his low estate, for none knoweth what his own end shall be.

Bahá'u'lláh, Gleanings from the Writings of Bahá'u'lláh, p. 265

I beg thee to forgive me 8

O my God, O my Lord, O my Master!
I beg Thee to forgive me
for seeking any pleasure save Thy love,
or any comfort except Thy nearness,
or any delight besides Thy good-pleasure
or any existence other than communion
with Thee.

The Báb, Selections from the Writings of the Báb, p. 215

Deal ye one with another   9

Deal ye one with another
with the utmost love and harmony,
with friendliness and fellowship.

Bahá'u'lláh, Epistle to the Son of the Wolf, p. 14

10   Enable me to grow

O Lord! I am a child; enable me to grow
beneath the shadow of Thy loving-kindness.
I am a tender plant; cause me to be nurtured
through the outpourings of the clouds of Thy
bounty. I am a sapling of the garden of love;
make me into a fruitful tree.
Thou art the Mighty and the Powerful,
and Thou art the All-Loving,
the All-Knowing, the All-Seeing.

'Abdu'l-Bahá, Bahá'í Prayers, p. 31

11 Generous in prosperity

Be generous in prosperity,
and thankful in adversity.

Bahá'u'lláh, Epistle to the Son of the Wolf, p. 93

Repair for refuge   12

O Lord! Unto Thee I repair for refuge, and toward all Thy signs I set my heart. O Lord! Whether traveling or at home, and in my occupation or in my work, I place my whole trust in Thee. Grant me then Thy sufficing help so as to make me independent of all things, O Thou Who art unsurpassed in Thy mercy! Bestow upon me my portion, O Lord, as Thou pleasest, and cause me to be satisfied with whatsoever Thou hast ordained for me. Thine is the absolute authority to command.

The Báb, Bahá'í Prayers, p. 55

Gentle winds  13

If it be Thy pleasure, make me to grow
as a tender herb in the meadows of Thy grace,
that the gentle winds of Thy will may stir me up
and bend me into conformity with Thy pleasure,
in such wise that my movement and my stillness
may be wholly directed by Thee.

Bahá'u'lláh, Prayers and Meditations by Bahá'u'lláh, p. 240

14 Thy name is my healing

Thy name is my healing, O my God,
and remembrance of Thee is my remedy.
Nearness to Thee is my hope,
and love for Thee is my companion.
Thy mercy to me is my healing and my succor
in both this world and the world to come.
Thou, verily, art the All-Bountiful,
the All-Knowing, the All-Wise.

Bahá'u'lláh, Bahá'í Prayers, p. 85

15 Benefit mankind

It behooveth man
to show forth
that which will benefit mankind.

Bahá'u'lláh, Epistle to the Son of the Wolf, p. 49

These lovely children 16

O Thou kind Lord!
These lovely children are the handiwork
of the fingers of Thy might
and the wondrous signs of Thy greatness.
O God! Protect these children,
graciously assist them to be educated and enable
them to render service to the world of humanity.
O God! These children are pearls, cause them to be
nurtured within the shell of Thy loving-kindness.
Thou art the Bountiful, the All-Loving.

'Abdu'l-Bahá, Bahá'í Prayers, p. 35

Blissful joy   17

Sorrow not if, in these days
and on this earthly plane,
things contrary to your wishes have been ordained
and manifested by God, for days of blissful joy,
of heavenly delight, are assuredly in store for you.

Bahá'u'lláh, Gleanings from the Writings of Bahá'u'lláh, p. 328

18   I have wakened

I have wakened in
Thy shelter, O my God, and it
becometh him that seeketh that shelter to
abide within the Sanctuary of Thy protection
and the Stronghold of Thy defense.
Illumine my inner being, O my Lord,
with the splendors of the Dayspring of Thy
Revelation, even as Thou didst illumine my
outer being with the morning
light of Thy favor.

Bahá'u'lláh, Bahá'í Prayers, p. 116

19 Kindly tongue

A kindly tongue is the lodestone
of the hearts of men.

Bahá'u'lláh, Epistle to the Son of the Wolf, p. 15

Aid Thou Thy trusted servants 20

O God, my God!
Aid Thou Thy trusted servants
to have loving and tender hearts.
Help them to spread, amongst all the nations
of the earth, the light of guidance that cometh
from the Company on high.
Verily, Thou art the Strong, the Powerful,
the Mighty, the All-Subduing,
the Ever-Giving. Verily, Thou art
the Generous, the Gentle,
the Tender, the Most Bountiful.

'Abdu'l-Bahá, Bahá'í Prayers, p. 173

Flame of love   21

Let the flame of the love of God
burn brightly within your radiant hearts.

Bahá'u'lláh, Gleanings from the Writings of Bahá'u'lláh, p. 325

22 Make Thy beauty

O my Lord! Make Thy
beauty to be my food,
and Thy presence my drink,
and Thy pleasure my hope,
and praise of Thee my action,
and remembrance of Thee my companion,
and the power of Thy sovereignty my succorer,
and Thy habitation my home,
and my dwelling-place the seat Thou hast
sanctified from the limitations imposed upon
them who are shut out as by a veil from Thee.
Thou art, verily, the Almighty,
the All-Glorious, the Most Powerful.

Bahá'u'lláh, Bahá'í Prayers, p. 143

23 Observe My commandments

Observe My commandments,
for the love of My beauty.

Bahá'u'lláh, The Kitáb-i-Aqdas, p. 20

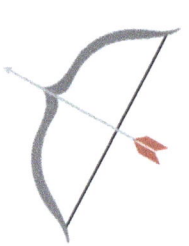

To be steadfast   24

O my Lord and my Hope!
Help Thou Thy loved ones
to be steadfast in Thy mighty Covenant,
to remain faithful to Thy manifest Cause,
and to carry out the commandments
Thou didst set down for them in Thy Book of Splendors;
that they may become banners of guidance and lamps
of the Company above,
wellsprings of Thine infinite wisdom,
and stars that lead aright, as they
shine down from the supernal sky.
Verily, Thou art the Invincible,
the Almighty, the All-Powerful.

'Abdu'l-Bahá, Bahá'í Prayers, p. 71

Be patient 25

Be patient under all conditions,
and place your whole trust
and confidence in God.

Bahá'u'lláh, Gleanings from the
Writings of Bahá'u'lláh, p. 296

26 Say: God sufficeth

Say: God sufficeth
all things above all things,
and nothing in the heavens
or in the earth
but God sufficeth.
Verily, He is in Himself
the Knower, the Sustainer,
the Omnipotent.

The Báb, Bahá'í Prayers, p. 27

27 Reconcile their differences

It is incumbent upon all the peoples of the world to reconcile their differences, and, with perfect unity and peace, abide beneath the shadow of the Tree of His care and loving-kindness.

Bahá'u'lláh, Gleanings from the Writings of Bahá'u'lláh, p. 6

Refresh and gladden 28

O God! Refresh and gladden my spirit.
Purify my heart. Illumine my powers.
I lay all my affairs in Thy hand.
Thou art my Guide and my Refuge.
I will no longer be sorrowful and grieved;
I will be a happy and joyful being.
O God! I will no longer be full of anxiety,
nor will I let trouble harass me.
I will not dwell on the unpleasant things of life.
O God! Thou art more friend to me than I am to myself.
I dedicate myself to Thee, O Lord.

Attributed to Ahmad Sohrab in Star of the West, vol 7, no. 18 (7 Feb 1917), p. 179

Sanctity of thy pledge 29

Be…a preserver of the
sanctity of thy pledge.

Bahá'u'lláh, Epistle to the Son of the Wolf, p. 93

30 Assist Thy loved ones

O Lord my God!
Assist Thy loved ones to be firm in Thy Faith,
to walk in Thy ways, to be steadfast in Thy Cause.
Give them Thy grace to withstand
the onslaught of self and passion,
to follow the light of divine guidance.
Thou art the Powerful, the Gracious,
the Self-Subsisting, the Bestower,
the Compassionate, the Almighty,
the All-Bountiful.

'Abdu'l-Bahá, Bahá'í Prayers, p. 165

31 Arise thou to serve

Arise thou to serve God
and help His Cause.

Bahá'u'lláh, Epistle to the Son of the Wolf, p. 47

I have detached myself 32

O my God, my Lord and my Master!
I have detached myself from my kindred
and have sought through Thee to become
independent of all that dwell on earth
and ever ready to receive
that which is praiseworthy in Thy sight.
Bestow on me such good as will make me
independent of aught else but Thee,
and grant me an ampler share
of Thy boundless favors.
Verily, Thou art the Lord of
grace abounding.

The Báb, Bahá'í Prayers, p. 19

Yield Him thanks 33

Reflect, O people, on the grace
and blessings of your Lord, and
yield Him thanks at eventide and dawn.

Bahá'u'lláh, The Kitáb-i-Aqdas, p. 30

34 Voice my thanks

My God, my Adored One, my King, my desire!
What tongue can voice my thanks to Thee?
I was heedless, Thou didst awaken me.
I had turned back from Thee,
Thou didst graciously aid me to turn towards Thee.
I was as one dead, Thou didst quicken me
with the water of life.
I was withered, Thou didst revive me
with the heavenly stream of Thine
utterance which hath flowed forth
from the Pen of the All-Merciful.

Bahá'u'lláh, Bahá'í Prayers, p. 18

35 Beautify your tongues

Beautify your tongues,
O people, with truthfulness,
and adorn your souls
with the ornament of honesty.

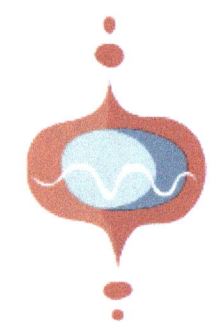

Bahá'u'lláh, Gleanings from the Writings of Bahá'u'lláh, p. 296

I am a little child 36

O Thou kind Lord! I am a little child,
exalt me by admitting me to the kingdom.
I am earthly, make me heavenly;
I am of the world below,
let me belong to the realm above;
gloomy, suffer me to become radiant;
material, make me spiritual,
and grant that I may manifest
Thine infinite bounties.
Thou art the Powerful, the All-Loving.

'Abdu'l-Bahá, Bahá'í Prayers, p. 35

Unity is firmly established 37

The well-being of mankind,
its peace and security,
are unattainable unless and until
its unity is firmly established.

Bahá'u'lláh, Gleanings from the Writings of Bahá'u'lláh, p. 286

38 Unite the hearts

O my God! O my God!
Unite the hearts of Thy servants,
and reveal to them Thy great purpose.
May they follow Thy commandments
and abide in Thy law. Help them, O God, in their
endeavor, and grant them strength to serve Thee.
O God! Leave them not to themselves,
but guide their steps by the light of Thy knowledge,
and cheer their hearts by Thy love.
Verily, Thou art their Helper and their Lord.

Bahá'u'lláh, Bahá'í Prayers, p. 203

39 Ayyám-i-Há Quotation

It behoveth the people of Bahá,
throughout these days, to provide good
cheer for themselves, their kindred and,
beyond them, the poor and needy,
and with joy and exultation
to hail and glorify their Lord,
to sing His praise and magnify His Name…

Bahá'u'lláh, The Kitáb-i-Aqdas, p. 25

My fire and my light — 40

My God, my Fire and my Light!
The days which Thou hast named
the Ayyám-i-Há in Thy Book
have begun, O Thou Who art the King
of names and the fast which Thy most
exalted Pen hath enjoined
unto all who are in the kingdom
of Thy creation to observe is approaching.

Bahá'u'lláh, Bahá'í Prayers, p. 235

Behind the Scenes - Recording the "At First Light" CD

List of Bahá'í Months

Gregorian Dates (when Naw-Rúz coincides with 21 March)	Arabic	English
21 March – 8 April	Bahá	Splendour
9 April – 27 April	Jalál	Glory
28 April – 16 May	Jamál	Beauty
17 May – 4 June	'Aẓamat	Grandeur
5 June – 23 June	Núr	Light
24 June – 12 July	Raḥmat	Mercy
13 July – 31 July	Kalimát	Words
1 August – 19 August	Kamál	Perfection
20 August – 7 September	Asmá'	Names

8 September – 26 September	'Izzat	Might
27 September – 15 October	Mashíyyat	Will
16 October – 3 November	'Ilm	Knowledge
4 November – 22 November	Qudrat	Power
23 November – 11 December	Qawl	Speech
12 December – 30 December	Masá'il	Questions
31 December – 18 January	Sharaf	Honour
19 January – 6 February	Sulṭán	Sovereignty
7 February – 25 February	Mulk	Dominion
26 February – 1 March	Ayyám-i-Há	The Days of Há
2 March – 20 March	'Alá'	Loftiness

For more "At First Light" resources visit SoulriseMelodies.com

www.ingramcontent.com/pod-product-compliance
Lightning Source LLC
Chambersburg PA
CBHW060520300426
44112CB00017B/2744